Believe Your Way to Success

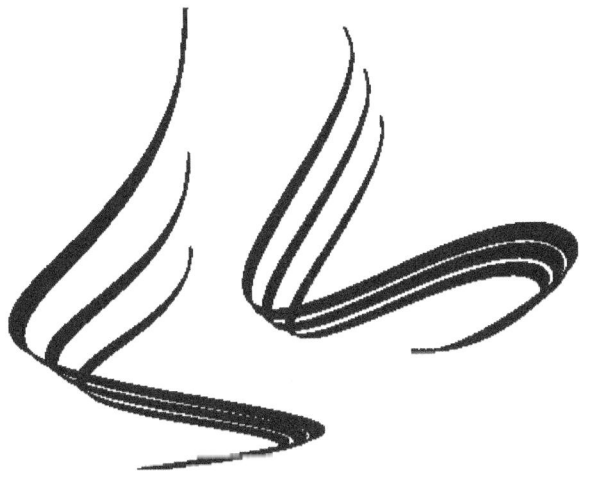

Believe Your Way to Success

The Definitive Guide to Believing and Your Path to Success

How Believing Takes You from Where You are to Where You Want to Be

Your Path to Success: A Five Part Series

Chase Andrews

Copyright © 2017 by Chase Andrews

All rights reserved. No part of this publication may be reproduced, distributed, or transmitted in any form or by any means, including photocopying, recording, or other electronic or mechanical methods, without the prior written permission of the publisher, except in the case of brief quotations embodied in critical reviews and certain other noncommercial uses permitted by copyright law. For permission requests, write to the publisher, addressed "Attention: Permissions Coordinator," at the address below.

Chase Andrews

chaseandrews@thepassiveincomemachine.com

www.thepassiveincomemachine.com

Make sure to check out the rest of the books in this series:

Fail Your Way to Success: The Definitive Guide to Failing Forward and Learning How to Extract the Greatness Within - Why Failing is an Integral Part of Success and Why You Should Never Fear it

https://www.amazon.com/dp/B0738WDK6W

Discipline Your Way to Success: The Definitive Guide to Success Through Self-Discipline - Why Self-Discipline is Crucial to Your Success Story and How to Take Control Over Your Thoughts and Actions

https://www.amazon.com/dp/B0741FMCBX

Meditate Your Way to Success: The Definitive Guide to Mindfulness, Focus and Meditation - How Meditation is an Integral Part of Success and Why You Should Get Started Now

https://www.amazon.com/dp/B073ZMCHQJ

Ask Your Way to Success: The Definitive Guide to Success Through Asking - How to Transform Your Life by Learning the Art of Asking

https://www.amazon.com/dp/B074CJPFMH

This book is dedicated to those of you who truly believe you were meant to be successful. You need to believe that anything and everything your mind can conjure up is possible, because it is.

Dare to believe…

Prologue
- Belief and Success

Preface
- The Ability to Believe
- The State of Belief

If

Introduction to the Power of Belief

Chapter 1: Self Doubt
- Smashing Self Doubt
- Rituals

Chapter 2: Procrastination
- Payoff, Output, and Probability

Chapter 3: Fear of Failure

Chapter 4: Excuses
- Use it

Chapter 5: Prejudice

Chapter 6: Negative Thoughts
- Vanquishing the Negative

Chapter 7: Pleasing Others

Chapter 8: Negative Environment

Chapter 9: Fear of Success

Chapter 10: Focusing on the Rewards

Conclusion

Epilogue

Invictus

Prologue

Success can be achieved by everyone. It is not discriminatory neither does it predetermine who can and cannot be successful. Success does not take into cognizance the place where you come from, or what you look like. It does not matter what your faith is: All that matters is what you believe. It does not matter what you did in the past; it matters only what you do at this moment. It doesn't matter if you fail a thousand times; it only matters if you get up to one thousand and one. It doesn't matter if you go wild at rave parties, bungee jump off bridges; as long as you realign your body, mind, and spirit.

Success is your right, and so is the freedom to pursue success or to languish in mediocrity. But I am guessing that you are tired of mediocrity and you want to change your current lot in life. Well, this is a good a place to start.

This is the fifth installment of a five part series on success. It is designed to give you an understanding of what success is, and what you need to see happen within you. It's not going to be a step-by-step guide because success is not a 3-step TV dinner. You don't just rip the shrink wrap, add water and place it in the microwave.

Each of you is different, and you will approach success from different backgrounds and with different motivations. If I gave you directions and steps to success, it would be like giving the same navigation instructions to get to Wichita, Kansas to two different guys, one in Boston and the other in Sacramento. But this book can tell you where success can be found, the means which you can use to find it, and have a go at it.

There are five cardinal elements in the body of success, all of which you need to master and internalize. The five, in equal importance, are:

- The ability to meditate for inspiration.
- The ability to learn from failure
- The ability to show discipline
- The ability to attract all you need by asking
- The ability to believe in yourself and your inspiration.

This book is about belief and how it relates to success

Before you embark on your journey through this book, whether you read the first four before getting here, or if this is your first introduction to the series, you should understand that this book is not sitting in front of you by chance. Somewhere along the line, your desire to explore a higher degree of success has brought this to you.

You are the embodiment of potential and the personification of all that is needed to impact this world and upgraded it to a better version of itself. Success is what we do in this physical world that adds to it: It is not something that we can do on our own. We need to be truly inspired. Success is not about copying something or mimicking something else. It's not about just combining two ideas and making a new one. All that is great, but the success you are capable of is a whole lot more.

I have come to believe that we are the nexus between the tangible and the intangible. Think about that for a minute. As I sit here, I am a tangible body endowed with the potential to be anything and to do anything. My inspiration is intangible and it comes to me by the law of attraction that is a vast field of energy we call the universe. From that inspiration that comes to me, I visualize things with my mind and make it happen with my hands. Suddenly, something that was not there can come into the present. From the nothingness, there is something, and that makes me the bridge between the two. You are no different.

To be able to succeed, you need to attract the universe and be a conduit for it. You have to pluck the ideas from the intangible and bring it to life here.

If you want to be successful, you have to ask for it. You must want it. You must attract it with all your being, and then it will come. It won't come pre-packaged and shiny- of course not. This isn't a game show where you win stuff out of sheer dumb luck. This is a reality. Here, you have to ask for it and when the universe responds, it does so with the presentation of opportunities. You have to take those opportunities and do something meaningful with them. That's how you make success and that's how you become great.

Belief and Success

We take belief for granted and at the same time, take success for granted as well. I will strongly advise that you stop doing that and take both of them very serious. If you do not pay attention to success, then distractions will rule and excellence would not be guaranteed. When distractions direct your actions, success will elude you and you will never understand why you can't achieve that level of success that you know you can reach deep inside. For those stuck in that limbo, life becomes bitter and painful. To truly lay the foundation of success within yourself, you need to apply the following five elements.

The first is the ability to understand failure and how failure can lead to success.

The second is to recognize and internalize discipline so that when your inspiration demands you to shift into top gear and put forward massive action, your body will do as your mind commands. The first two books set the stage for success and what it means, and why you shouldn't shortchange yourself as to the height of your success.

The third is the power of meditation that you need to understand your place and purpose in the world so that you can go on to leverage who you are and bear fruits of greatness.

The fourth is that you must understand the role of asking and how asking for what you want, does not start and stop at your lip but vibrates within the silence of your meditation. The fourth element that is needed is the ability to ask and a strong grasp of what to ask for. People are often astounded by how simple the notion of asking really is. We sometimes choose not to ask, because subconsciously, we are not ready for success, or we are in fear of it. If you can't ask for success, then it should occur to you that there is some form of baggage that you need to jettison, and that can be taken care of by means of meditation and reflection. Asking is an art that you need to internalize. As simple as it sounds, many people lose the ability and the inclination to ask for what they want. Asking helps to clarify both the start of your journey and its course. Whatever you ask for, the Universe will reply in provision of opportunities.

Finally, there is the element of belief, which is the focus of this book. You need to believe that anything and everything is possible. You need to believe that what you will embark on will yield a positive result in the making of your success and the reaching of your greatness.

This series on success takes the information you need to find the potential in you, and helps you to manifest the success you are born to achieve. The material is laid out across five books, ideally, read in sequence.

i. Fail Your Way to Success
ii. Discipline Your Way to Success
iii. Meditate Your Way to Success
iv. Ask Your Way to Success
v. Believe Your Way to Success

To approach the gates of success in its entirety, you will have to lay assault on the hordes of ignorance multiple times, reflect on the meaning of success, and weed out the negative mindset that has prevented you from the things that you need to embrace. You will be surprised to see how the same lines can have a deeper impact each subsequent time you come at it until you get to a point that the information becomes fluid and your own truth emerges from it.

The result should be a visceral understanding of what success is and what you need to do.

***

Preface

"Be fearless in the pursuit of what sets your soul on fire."

Anonymous

When someone describes how their soul is inflamed by a particular thing, it means that they are inspired. That inspiration comes from the well of the universe governed by the Laws of Attraction.

Success is merely the fruition of something that started as an inspiration, transmitted to you by the universe, cogitated by your mind, and worked on by your hands.

Your true starting point to achieving success and greatness is inspiration. Without true inspiration, nothing worthy is possible. It is not your mind that conjures the non-existent. If something doesn't exist in physical or logical form, the mind is incapable of taking the leap to the next iteration. But inspiration doesn't come from the mind, contrary to popular belief, it comes to us from the universe via the soul.

Of course, advancing from one microchip at lower processing capability to the next generation chip with higher capability is the fruit of a brilliant mind. The brain is good at that because it knows how to learn new stuff and contemplate the next step through critical thinking. It knows how to envision in incremental improvements.

Incremental ideas are the products of the mind, but the genesis of the original idea is, and always will be, the inspiration of your soul.

To be truly successful, you need to be able to bring forth that inspiration from within. Not just once or twice in your life, but numerous times and in varying forms. Your ability to be inspired, stay inspired and peek into the world that does not yet exist, is within you, **don't doubt that**.

In the grand scheme of things, your life does not only comprise of your breathing and walking. Rather, your life is a contribution to the world. If you were to stand atop a fictional mountain and shout out to the entire world, "$E = MC^2$", the world shout back, "Albert Einstein".

Shout "light bulb", and they would return "Thomas Edison";

For "telephone", it would be "Alexander Graham Bell";

For airplanes, the Wright Brothers;

For printing press, Johannes Gutenberg; and there would be thousands upon thousands of other pairings of contribution and person one could come up with, but only one should be important to you: Yours.

What can you do to get the world to shout your name?

What is your contribution to the world? What is it that takes your life and makes it as it should be? What's going to make you great? The greatness you seek is already residing within you. But you are also endowed with one more gift - the gift of true freewill. What you do with your life is entirely up to you. You can sink to the depths of depravity, or you can rise to the level of the stars.

Where you are right now, is not a matter of the fates - it's you. Every single failure in your life that remained a failure is because you chose not to get back up: No one stopped you. It was the same for me. It is the same for everybody. No big secret there so stop making excuses.

Until I stopped making excuses and took responsibility for my own state, success was always in view but never in hand. This, I see time and time again in many people I meet during the course of my daily events. Let me tell you that every idea you have is either an opportunity or a distraction. But every clear inspiration you have is an opportunity to fulfill a desire that you harbor inside. All you have to do is sharpen that desire, focus on the inspiration, hunker down, and get to work. That's all it takes.

Why then are you not as successful as you can be? The answer is simple - it's because you don't believe.

The contribution that you make does not have to be an invention, it can be anything. It can be art, sculpture, stories, processes, methods or just about anything else. However, whatever you choose to create must greatly impact the quality of lives around you. There are two ways you can advance swiftly on the path to your success and contribution.

The first is by understanding how the inspiration, which you get to do something, comes. For some people, they just wake up one day and have the burning desire to contribute something to the world. For others, they know they want to succeed but don't know where to get their ideas from.

One excellent way to get them is through meditation. As you refine your ability to focus, be mindful, and slowly calm the waters of your mind, you will begin to experience the state of meditation.

It has been proven by successful CEOs and high-energy entrepreneurs that meditation not only reduces stress but also induces creativity in solving problems and challenges. Meditation is the gateway to getting in touch with the part of you that is connected to the universe. Meditation activates that part of you that resonates at a frequency that attracts the opportunities you need to make your desires take flight. It is a crucial step that you neglect at your own peril; All because you don't believe.

Meditation is not religious; so for those of you who have strong faith in your practices, you are not transgressing any tenet of your religion. Meditation is not about chanting. Meditation is not about subscribing to Hindu or Buddhist values and teachings. It is true that Buddhists and Hindus use meditation as part of their spiritual exercises, but meditation is meditation just as genuflecting is just genuflecting. Just like the fact that genuflecting doesn't make you Catholic, meditation has no religious connotation just because a particular religion may use it. I know some people are afraid to meditate because they think that it is a domain of a particular religious practice; it's not.

Pursue the art of meditation so that you can tap from the energy residing within you. That energy is the same energy that makes up the fabric of the universe and when you tap from it, all that you need, whether it is inspiration or guidance, will be provided by the universe.

Once you have the inspiration you need, you can move on to pursue the creation and conversion of the intangible into tangible results. It is wholly insufficient to be satisfied with just the inspiration, you must take it to the next level by making it materialize. However, it is a pity that most people get the inspiration but don't act on it because they don't believe they have what it takes to channel it towards materialization. They either don't believe in themselves, or they don't believe in the genuineness of their inspiration: at worse, they believe that trying and failing is going to make them look silly and not worth the effort.

This book is all about believing, which really does cover a lot of ground. Belief, as it relates to success, is a three-dimensional construct that you cannot see, hear or touch. It is intangible and pervades both your soul and your mind. It is the gatekeeper of your psyche and the protector of your soul.

The intangible force of energy is wholly misunderstood to be something more of an acquiescent state where people take a passive role like a child buys into the reality of a stick figure animation. Belief is nothing like that. Instead, belief is a force that you emanate outward, which shows that you are in total control.

Belief is the energy that allows you to shape-shift. The moment you apply the power of belief to something, you will shift your entire being and take the shape necessary to advance.

The Ability to Believe

The ability to believe is a function of three variables. It is directly proportional to your mindful state. The more mindful you are, the more you will believe in the things that advance you and disbelieve the things that distract you. Your natural instinct will protect you from events that serve to derail you if you develop and sharpen your ability to be aware and mindful of yourself and your goals.

The second variable is the core strength that you build. The stronger you are, the more you are able to believe in your own ability and be less afraid of the unknown. Without this strength, your fear will rise to the surface making you doubt your inspiration and relegating every thought of success to an early grave. As human beings, we naturally fear the unknown. This inherent fear of all things unknown can trip you up because, to really succeed, we have to go where no man has gone before. To succeed you have to come face to face with the unknown and that precipitates fear. But for you to overcome and leave concrete imprints on the sands of time, you cannot afford to give into fear because fear will knock you off your footing. To stand up to fear, you must build strength in the form of belief in yourself and all you do.

The third variable is an in-depth knowledge of you. Here, you need to engage in self introspection. Be true to yourself about what you know, what you don't, and where your strength and weaknesses lay. As Shakespeare writes, *"To thine own self be true."*

There are two parts to this. On the one hand, you must have high confidence that you can achieve anything, and on the other hand, you must also be humble enough to realize the truth is that you don't know everything.

Most people misunderstand these two parts. They are afraid of what they don't know and confuse that with thinking that their potential is flawed. Not knowing something is only temporary: Knowing that thing is forever. Only you can decide if you will allow your ignorance to be permanent or temporary. If you apply will and discipline, you can acquire the knowledge that will vanquish the ignorance.

This third element is the knowledge of yourself and filling in the gaps when necessary. The third element of your belief must be this ability to see yourself in truth and transparency. If you hide your shortfalls to satisfy your ego, there will always be a part of you that is uncertain of your footing because you know beneath the surface that you are lacking in a certain area. As such this third element is about truth and transparency.

Just to a quick recap - the first variable element of belief is mindfulness. As you vary the level of mindfulness, all else being equal, you impact your ability to believe proportionately. The second variable is strength, where the stronger you are, the higher your power of belief. Finally, the variable of knowing the truth and being transparent to yourself. The more transparent you are, the more powerful your belief.

The State of Belief

Your level of success is directly proportional to the state of your belief. The state of your belief is the summation of the three elements described in the above section.

If you are strong willed in self-confidence and stand up to your fear, and if at the same time you are mindful and aware of yourself and your desires, you will find that the resulting state you are in is one of strong belief in yourself and in the final outcome of your inspiration.

When you have this belief and you fail at something, you will have no doubt in your mind that you can get up and get back to work. The belief you have, fortifies you from within and you need that kind of fortification to be able to succeed and it carries you to greatness. You have to manage this state of belief consistently.

Your state of belief is not something you can reach by accident. It doesn't happen by chance and it can be eroded if you are not in careful cognizance of its power. You have to guard your belief, and in the event you feel unsure, you need to examine the elements that go into strengthening and defining your belief.

The above is an incontestable fact. What you believe in will always be your reality, regardless of what others choose to tell you. If you believe that you will never amount to much, you're right. But if you believe, even with evidence to the contrary, that you will be wildly successful, you will be right as well. As Henry Ford said, *"Whether you think you can, or you think you can't, you're right."*

All else being equal, it does not matter how educated you are, how much you inherited, or where you are born. What you need is to believe that you can be whatever you want to be. The other side of that coin is that you will be whatever you are afraid of being. Between the both outcomes, what do you think determines the one that materializes in the tangible world?

Is it belief?

No. This is a trick question because you will end up being whichever you apply the more energy to. Belief is a form of energy, and so is fear, if regulated incorrectly.

Many people end up becoming exactly what they fear. Look at it this way, whatever you pay attention to is what will materialize in your life. That's where elders talk about bad luck when they say talking about bad things could result in it happening. It's not bad luck, it's about your state of belief.

***

If
by Rudyard Kipling

If you can keep your head when all about you
Are losing theirs and blaming it on you,
If you can trust yourself
when all men doubt you
But make allowance for their doubting too,
If you can wait and not be tired by waiting,
Or being lied about, don't deal in lies,
Or being hated, don't give way to hating,
And yet don't look too good, nor talk too wise:

If you can dream –
and not make dreams your master.
If you can think –
and not make thoughts your aim;
If you can meet with Triumph and Disaster
And treat those two impostors just the same;
If you can bear to hear the truth you've spoken
Twisted by knaves to make a trap for fools,
Or watch the things you gave your life to, broken,
And stoop and build them up
with worn-out tools:

If you can make one heap of all your winnings
And risk it all on one turn of pitch-and-toss,
And lose, and start again at your beginnings

And never breathe a word about your loss;

If you can force your heart
and nerve and sinew
To serve your turn long after they are gone,
And so hold on when there is nothing in you
Except the will which says to them: "Hold on!"

If you can talk with crowds
and keep your virtue,
Or walk with kings –
nor lose the common touch,
If neither foes nor loving friends can hurt you;
If all men count with you, but none too much,
If you can fill the unforgiving minute
With sixty seconds' worth of distance run,
Yours is the Earth and everything that's in it,
And—which is more--you'll be a Man, my son.

Introduction to the Power of Belief

The road to success has many detours and distractions. Among the lot of them, I've chosen ten of the most common to reveal their nature and how belief is the best way to overcome them:

I. Self-doubt
II. Procrastination
III. Fear of Failure
IV. Excuses
V. Prejudice
VI. Negative Thoughts
VII. Pleasing Others
VIII. Negative Environment
IX. Fear of Success
X. Focusing on the Rewards

Every single one of these detours can be fatal to the attainment of success because they represent the manifestation of our inability to believe in our own abilities. You may even think that you are not worthy of success and that a mediocre life is all you need to get by. None of that is true. You have the free will to desire success, you have the universe which you have equal right to extract inspiration, and you have the free will to use your body and mind to make that inspiration a reality.

The following ten chapters will cover each detour in turn so that you may be able to understand the detour when you are faced with it, and you will uncover the level of belief you need to invoke upon reaching the detour to get past it.

By this point, you may have had the opportunity to read the preceding four books covering the other four elements needed to succeed. The one additional thing you need to know is that these are not rigid frameworks like a scaffold at a construction site where you lay one something on top of the other and voila! you have a platform.

That's not how it works.

What you really have to do is develop each skill individually. Once you understand them, you have to assemble each and with all five, you can now build one atop of each other. What you will find is that each element becomes richer by its combination with the others. It's an iterative collaboration as each element comes together and mixes with the other; they boost their characters and the whole is much greater than the individual parts.

Once you get to that level, you will see that you don't need to give your effort a second look. You will find that you are always geared up and always ready to rumble. Success, at that point, becomes second nature.

That's the way we have evolved. If you take away the distractions, success is in our nature. But we have been blinded and become part of a collective that looks like something out of the Matrix trilogy - plugged in and doped up to be content with a simple existence. Our real nature is that of a highly successful life, designed for greatness, but unfortunately, distracted by sideshows.

***

Chapter 1: Self Doubt

"It's not what you think that's holding you back, it's what you think you are not."

Anonymous

At the top of the list of things that will throw a cog into your entire plan to be successful, is the seeming unexpected feeling of self-doubt. While you don't plan on it and certainly don't want it, you should never fall into the trap of thinking that self-doubt is not something that is beyond you. It is, and it can surface at a time when you least expect.

Self-doubt will throw you off your game, whether it's in a bar room pool game or Olympic swimming competition. It's a condition that creeps up upon you on the eve of battle and questions your entire existence and right to stand at the cusp of success. You can curse it, you can hate it, and you can fear it, but it's pointless because self-doubt is not real. It's not real as in, it's not tangible and not something that is grounded in reality or truth. It is grounded, however, deep within your psyche.

Self-doubt that attacks moments before the finish line can only be managed. There are tactics and strategies to quell self-doubt at the moment it occurs before a duel or competition. These tactics can typically be breathing exercises that are similar to mindfulness training. We will discuss tactics later on in this chapter.

The time to totally expunge self-doubt is before it strikes. The removal of self-doubt should be an exercise that you undertake in your run up to success and in your outside life – that is the leisure time that is not related to the work that you do to achieve the success that you envision.

There are a number of levels of self-doubt. Some come in the form of questions and they challenge your worthiness to succeed at the tasks you are doing: others come to you in the form of disbelief that you are indeed destined to take the glory you deserve. There are some people who even succeed once and then feel guilty about their success so much so that they never attempt to succeed again. The self doubt makes them feel like frauds and that they may be found out.

Experiences dating back to the time you were a child show that self-doubt may have began with you being told that you are not good enough, or that you cannot do anything: on the other hand, strong belief may have been built up when parents and the environment encourage you positively. There are many psychological reasons that could point to this, but it is not a unique phenomenon, neither is it one that is rarely found. Self-doubt is a widespread issue among many people who, under normal circumstances, seem confident and gregarious.

The reason you experience self-doubt is that you lack the basic understanding of the universe and your role in it. You do not comprehend that nature of life and the nature of the universe that supports this life. You may not understand your contribution to it and how your presence in this world, and the things that you do, has an impact on all the things that happen around you, and that wave of change moves across the world.

The larger the potential of your success, the stronger the wave it will create and the farther it will reach in time and space. In the last book, you learned about the balance of the tangible and the intangible. To be able to push back and annihilate self-doubt, you need to sharpen your understanding and your ability to use tangible actions to push back the intangible self defeating thoughts.

Self-doubt is the manifestation of the psyche's fear of change. When you go from one unsuccessful state to the cusp of a successful one, the part of you that is not used to success is going to fear the sudden change. You must always remember that the mind is always afraid of things that it is not familiar with. This fear of the unfamiliar manifests at the point when you are about to change your state of being- from being a mediocre person to someone successful. You will eventually have the same fear when you begin to move up from one level of success to another. Just like Alexander and each war that closely brought him to acquiring the whole of Europe.

There are many kinds of fear, even some that are designed to protect you. Sometimes, even the fear of the unknown may be there to protect you because, on the balance of probability, the unknown may hold dangers that you are not prepared for. Statistically, it is better to not traverse the unknown because the content may be profitable or detrimental. So for this reason, it raises the flag of caution that truly cloaks fear. That is one face of self-doubt.

The second face of self-doubt is actually rooted in laziness. Because a change in state requires greater energy, the body is not willing to expend the energy and would rather see you stay still and conserve that energy for future use. There is nothing as comforting as staying put in our comfort zone. As short-sighted as it may sound, one must remember the body strives to survive at all costs. The body is not interested in success or greatness; rather, it has one objective, and that objective doesn't care about success or greatness. In fact, the pursuit of success is sometimes at odds with the body's purpose, so it actually has a reason to fight it.

As you propel yourself towards the achievement of repeated success, the body slowly learns that success can be beneficial to it as well. All this while, before reaching a measure of success, the body felt that you were taking away from it and the body built up a resistance to counter such efforts. But once you get beyond that stage and you began to succeed and the success brought with it rewards that the body enjoyed, it starts to get on board. That's one of the reasons people who are successful find it easier to attain lateral successes.

Smashing Self Doubt

You must smash self-doubt at its genesis and not let it fester and trigger at a later date. To do this you need to come to the realization that you are worthy of success and that your mind, body, and soul can all be geared towards greatness.

That is your first step. Without coming to this realization, most people will experience bouts of self-doubt when they approach success. The only weapon to defeat self-doubt so that its seed never sprouts, is to make certain that your belief is formidable and there is no chink in the armor.

Of course, absolute certainty against self-doubt takes time to build and you may arrive at moments when the doubts will arise. However, there are simple things you can do to surmount the bumps that present themselves as self-doubt on your road to success. The first is that you must handle them before you experience the self-doubt at the cusp of success.

You should take the effort to understand that you will be changing your personality and that change is not to be feared. This is the point where you have to believe that you are worthy of success. If you believe you are worthy, and you believe that all of us, not just you, are worthy of success, then you will not feel alien when you are about to change your state from being mediocre to successful.

You have to believe that only good will arise from this process and that with it, you can do more good. That good comes at the price of your effort and that nothing can trip you up because what you are doing is the best outcome for you, your family and the world at large.

Rituals

Tangible actions to ward off intangible state of self doubt are called rituals. You've seen them with every successful athlete from Jordan to Schumacher. For instance, Wade Boggs, Hall of Fame Yankee third basemen, would do the exact same three things before every game to cast off the jitters and increase his 'luck'.

At exactly 5:17 pm on the evening of a night game, he would begin his batting practice, and then at exactly 7:17 pm, he would commence his wind sprints. After all these, he has a chicken dinner, which is a must on game day.

None of this is crazy and everyone who is successful has had some form of ritual at some point in their life.

For me, my ritual was simple and on the days I didn't get to my ritual, I was convinced that I was off my game. This seemed to show in my attitude towards work; it showed up in my sessions; and it showed up in my negotiations.

My ritual used to be that I woke up at exactly 5:11 every morning and started my day by making a fresh cup of ginger tea. I used to stir it exactly 32 times, then followed that with an exercise regimen that consisted of a number of routines before sitting down to meditate and then hitting the shower and getting into a fresh white shirt. Every day that I did this, I was on top of the world. It gave me the strength to do anything. I felt invincible. I felt successful and believed that I could do anything.

I don't do these rituals anymore. Something else came along in my life and displaced the need for rituals to energize the core beliefs in myself. After setting goals beyond my reach and achieving each one of them, the feeling of self-doubt has gradually vanished from my range of feelings. These days, I work on my inspiration without question, I am thrilled to get started on a new idea or excited to incorporate my latest inspiration into my current goal.

This book is anchored in the power of belief. Self-doubt is just the first of ten hurdles that belief effectively and appropriately vanquishes. The interesting thing about self-doubt is that you can actually use it to build your belief. Think of self-doubt as a sparring partner the next time it surfaces and find the power of your belief in yourself and in your mission and stare your self-doubt down.

***

Chapter 2: Procrastination

"Procrastination is opportunity's assassin"

Victor Kiam

Have you ever procrastinated in anything? Think back to any point in time, and ponder over the things you procrastinated about. Over the course of my study of success, I have repeatedly observed that procrastination typically emerges when you are not so interested in the thing that you are putting off.

Usually, if I want something and I believe it's as easy to reach and achieve, I just do it and within moments, I have it in my hand. There is no procrastinating involved. However, there are times when I do not believe that the goal I am aspiring to, can be easily attained. There are also times when the goal I wish to attain seems plausible, but the amount of energy that goes into it is so high that the payoff doesn't seem worth the effort. What happens next is that I put off such goals to a time when the stars may align better and I don't have to put so much into it or the chances of achievement are higher. In a nutshell, these are the basis of procrastination.

To be successful, you need to know the limits of your body, and the one thing you need to totally get on board with is that there is a reason your body does what it does and reacts the way it does; None of it is random. The more you know yourself, the better you will be able to answer its concerns and get your body to get on board the ride to the achievement of your goals.

From the body's perspective, procrastination and laziness have one purpose which is to conserve the body's resources in any straining endeavor. The body doesn't know the payoff any particular action will yield, so when you try something new, it has no benchmark to gauge what the payoff may be. Hence, when it doesn't recognize that benchmark, it assumes the worst and you feel the laziness creep in. When you do this, the body rewards you with endorphins and the laziness feels good.

The body is tasked with one purpose alone (you should read the other books in this Success series to understand the dual purpose of the self) and that purpose is to live and to extend your genes to the next generation. That's its highest priority. In keeping up with its purpose, it needs to be able to conserve and use energy over the course of its life. To do that the body either has to eat more, which sometimes results in being overweight; or it chooses to conserve energy, which manifests in laziness and procrastination.

There are two ways to get over this insidious hurdle.

- The first is to understand the power of now. In conducting mindfulness exercises, you will slowly begin to understand the power of now. The power of now overshadows the sense of urgency and thoughts of future pay off. There's a greater power at play when you do things in the present moment. You can only experience that when you get used to it. There is only one way to change your future and that way resides in the present. How you act now echoes through into the future and it is the only tool to change the future.

You cannot step into the future without passing the gate of the present, and that is where your mind ought to be. **You cannot change your life by visiting the past because you can't go back there and change it.** Your only opportunity to make yourself a success in the future is to work the present.

To be able to do things in the present, you need to constantly wrestle control of the body from the body's systems and deploy it toward the tasks that the mind sets in motion. This can be difficult, but I guarantee you that the mind does have final say on what the body does, you just have to be firm about this.

- The second is to ramp up your power to believe in your inspiration and in yourself. When you combine belief and mindfulness, not only does it vanquish any form of procrastination, it expedites your track to success.

When I first began my quest to find ways to counter procrastination, I had to look closely at what my body was saying when it decided to put tasks off, and when it decided to jump to it. I noticed that things that I wanted or was originally motivated to do, come without any resistance especially when I had done it previously and the win was easy.

However, at times when the win was a struggle, my body kept trying to put it off to later. The low hanging fruit was a no-brainer. The higher the fruit, the more effort it takes, and the less the certainty of quick payoff, the higher the body's tendency to find excuses.

I then noticed that there was a myriad of reasons that determined how easy or difficult my body made it for me to be able to do something.

There are three factors in general. They may be the same for you, or they may vary. You have to take note of your own system and sort out which part of you is making the demands. In my case the three areas were:

I. Payoff
II. Energy output
III. Potential of failure (probability)

Payoff, Output, and Probability

The body works on corporal economic foundation that is very concerned with payoff. Every endeavor needs to have a payoff that goes towards fulfilling its purpose. You remember that we mentioned earlier in the series that the body's purpose is to live and extend life to the next generation. In pursuit of this, energy is the commodity that it weighs in relation to any chore. How much energy does it have to spend and how much energy can it get in return.

So let's say they are giving away free cupcakes at the store a mile away. Each cupcake yields 120 calories and it takes your body 100 calories to make the trip (you don't need to worry about the trip back because you'll be seeing your buddy there who is going to give you a ride back in his car). So in this equation, you net 20 calories. The certainty of getting the cupcake when you get there is 100%. So, your body decides, all else being equal, that it's worth making the journey, and there would be no need to procrastinate.

But let's say, the trip back was now uncertain because your buddy only has a 20% chance of being there and he hasn't promised you that he will give you a ride back. What happens now? Your body gets a little uncertain if it wants to make the trip because there is a possibility that you end up expending 200 calories for a 120 calorie payoff. Corporal economics looks at this as a bad bet and delays action- till things can get a little more certain. So in the meantime, you just don't 'feel' like making the trip.

To be able to battle procrastination, you must take two steps. The first step is that you must understand your inspiration and believe in what you can do and that the universe never steers you wrong.

The second step is that you reward your body in a direct and appealing way that the body understands. This is especially effective if you are new to the success game. When you are new, the body doesn't get your long term goals and it doesn't get the value of success.

The bottom line is simple. Your body wants to be rewarded for its efforts in a currency that goes directly to its sustainability. We talk primarily about energy, but there are other factors besides energy that figure into this complex calculus. The currency is basically the aggregate of anything and everything that gets to keep the body living and the second it sees anything that gets its genes to pass to the next generation - which relates to attracting a mate and also protecting that family. Everything that leads to those objectives is a currency the body is willing to accept – (when we say body, remember it is actually a part of the primal brain that is doing this. It is easy to say 'body' for illustration purposes).

Belief is the conqueror of procrastination. The stronger and more robust your belief, the less the body will throw up procrastination in response to a command you issue. You strengthen your belief in your inspiration and in your ability to make that inspiration materialize. Make sure that the body is rewarded in incremental steps and in shorter intervals.

***

Chapter 3: Fear of Failure

"It's not failure itself that holds you back; it's the fear of failure that paralyzes you."

Brian Tracy

In the top ten lists of reasons why people never even start to get the fire that inspires them, the fear of failure ranks at the top three. This is not some gremlin in the night. It is a legitimate failure and doesn't let anyone tell you that those fears are irrelevant. They are relevant, but not in the way you think. Their relevance is not about what you should be afraid of, but the deficiency that is causing you to drag your feet.

You make use of the fear of failure, not to inform you that the possibility of fear is there, rather, you use that fear to inform you that you can't stop until you get to your goal. You have to tell yourself that the higher the purpose and the more the initiative, the higher the chances of failure and you have to just make sure you get up and try again. Until you believe in yourself, the fear of failure will present a self-fulfilling prophecy that you will keep falling and the only cure that will change that is when you begin to believe.

When I was four, my father came home one evening after work with a shiny new bicycle. Yes, it had training wheels, which gave me the sense of security I needed to get on and not fear the fall. I think I was more concerned with looking foolish than bruising my knee.

The many times I got on the bike in his presence slowly got me to realize that it was a lot of fun and a big change from the tricycle that I'd had from even before I could remember. Hence, the training wheels stayed on for a couple of months. After some time my father started hinting at getting the training wheels off but that fell on deaf years. When he started telling me directly, I just declined, insisted and went to a higher power for backup - my mother.

Eventually one evening, he came back and just started removing the training wheels and told me that it was time and that I would be surprised if I just let myself do it. I remember him telling me that he believed I was ready and that he wouldn't let go of me and that there was nothing to worry about.

I took his word for it, and he got behind me and started pushing. It was a blast; I can still remember it after all this time. If I close my eyes, I can almost feel the wind on my face, the smell of the grass and my father's voice just inches above me, assuring me that he was right there.

We went around in big circles, all the while he kept pushing me from behind, and not once did I fall. His encouragement and the evidence that the training wheels were unnecessary, got my confidence up and I was feeling great about myself.

My dad was better than any pair of training wheels, and my mom was standing there anytime we began: each time I went one full circuit she would stand there and cheer me on. I don't know how many times we did this, or when he stopped whispering because I was busy peddling and having fun until I came up to where my mom was standing, and to my surprise, my dad was standing right there next to her. He had let go and he had let me ride all on my own and I did it. Four and a half years old, and I was riding without training wheels and without my dad.

The only thing stopping me from taking off the training wheels earlier was my fear of failure. I didn't like the idea of falling because I didn't know how badly I would be injured but I was less afraid of falling than of looking silly.

It turns out that most of us view life with the exact same lenses. We are afraid not just of the consequence of failure, but we are also afraid of looking silly. This is the real problem because the consequences of failure are minimal.

We can always recover and what's more, failure is a great way of teaching the body and the mind the extent of things or the right way of doing things. **Failure is never final**. What kills us is the time when we refuse to get back up. The real assassin is not the failure; it's our own mind that prevents us from trying again.

We fear to look silly, we fear the unknown, and we fear consequences that we cannot fathom. Because of this, the moment we get to a comfortable place along our path to success, we cash in and settle for a mediocre life. That's really how the fear of failure gets you; it's by telling you to give up early.

The only way to counter any of this is for you to believe that failure is a good thing because it teaches you what you don't know about yourself and about the thing you are attempting.

Each time you fail, the universe is telling you the path not to take. The best lesson of failure has been the story of Edison's ten thousand attempts at creating the light bulb. He says it perfectly in the end. He said, *"I didn't fail ten thousand times, I just found ten thousand ways not to do it"*. That is the essence of failure that we need to realize. Our fear of failure can be easily surmounted by believing that not only will our body, mind, and spirit rise to the challenge after falling a few times, but what's more is that inspiration is every bit as achievable in reality as it is to walk to the corner store.

Edison's inspiration for the incandescent light bulb was spot on, and by the process of elimination, he eventually found how to make it a reality. He just believed in it every step of the way.

Belief is the strongest reaction you can have to any hurdle that lies in your way. Build that belief in your inspiration and in yourself, and protect it with the might of your strength. Belief is the thing that will see you through the darkest nights and the harshest storms. Just hold on and, after the first few times, you will find that it will become second nature.

***

Chapter 4: Excuses

"Excuses are what your lips make when your hands can't make what your soul dreams of. The biggest problem with excuses is not that you let anyone down; it's that you let your own soul down. "

Anonymous

A thousand years ago, some guy was inspired to do something but instead of making it, he made excuses. History has forgotten him, you and I don't know who that even is. He lays now in the mass graves of the unknown. His tombstone may as well read *"Purveyor of Fine Excuses"*

I refuse to let that happen to me. I refuse to spend my life on this earth and leave it being well known as the purveyor of excuses. I refuse to betray my soul and the universe by walking away from my inspiration and instead, using my precious time in making excuses. What about you?

Early in my twenties, I was very driven. There was a lot of raw energy and I used to go out and achieve things just because I could. I had no idea where the inspiration came from and no idea what I believed in. All I knew was that I wanted something, and I just didn't stop till I got it. However, there were a few things that would bring me to my knees- my Achilles heel, if you would say. If I had a deadline of Tuesday, or Sunday to submit a proposal on a bid I was working on, I had a vicious migraine. I automatically would coil up and start popping aspirin and go in search of a dark room to fall asleep and come back to the world once the migraine had left.

I did the same thing this time, and I realized that this was a habit with me. I had never tried to do anything about my migraine and I never tried to surmount it. So, Sunday came and went and I spent it asleep all day and all night. When I woke up Monday morning at 4:11 am, to my surprise the pulsing migraine was there and it was debilitating. I had just 24 hours to get the proposal done and had no room for wasted time. This prompted my decision, for the first time ever, to push through my migraine, and get to work. I went through my morning rituals and I made a stand that I had to do what needed to be done.

The proposal went out on time and we secured the bid eventually, but the greatest victory I had that day was that I had learned something monumentally valuable. I learned that excuses aren't just implausible reasons for not doing something; excuses are anything you tell yourself when you detract from your goal, no matter how real it may seem. That migraine was a valid reason for me to deviate from my actions; but the moment I classified it as an excuse and disregarded it, I was able to move on.

I've seen it time and again in winners. One example that has gone on to solidify my stand on this is a Formula 1 race that happened in 2003 on the Italian circuit in Imola. It is about Michael Schumacher, one of the world's greatest F1 drivers and seven-time Champion (no other driver has won the Championship seven times, and no one has won it five times in a row).

Schumacher's mother, whom he was very close to, had been admitted to the hospital in a coma. She was near her end at the time. After paying his last respects, Michael returned to the circuit in Imola, Italy, and prepared for the race. Only a few hours before the race was flagged off, he received news that his mother had passed. Anyone would have accepted that as a valid reason if Michael had stepped aside from that race. He didn't. As devastated as he was, he got in his car and went on to complete the race and more importantly, won it. He went on to win the Championship that year; his fourth in a row.

Excuses are the wall that the weak lean on. They rely on excuses to camouflage their inability to believe in their own ability and in their dreams. When they indulge in excuses, they give themselves an escape hatch. It is indeed the weak who use excuses and it is indeed strength in belief that can erase the need for excuses.

When you believe something can be done, you will never allow anything to come in-between its actualization. You see the opportunity so starkly when it comes to low hanging fruit that you have no excuses and you just take what is in front of you, because your belief is not diluted by thoughts of probability, thoughts of failure, or thoughts of looking stupid: none of those matter one iota compared to the assault that you lay on your prize and the attainment of victory.

Use it

Instead of letting excuses derail your efforts, study it and its origins. You need to do this when you reflect on your actions. One of the things that I observe successful people do, is that they always conduct postmortems of their frame of mind and actions. In other words, they spend once a day reflecting on things that they have done or things that have come into their life.

People who are just starting out with reflection do it to look back on their day to learn how to react better to things that happened to them. That is a great place to start. But for those of us who have been doing this for a while, reflection is a powerful tool to understand yourself. In the case of excuses, use it to determine the level of belief you have in your idea and try to understand what part of you doesn't have the belief that what you are doing is worthy of your time and effort.

When you analyze this, what you are doing is merely trying to understand yourself and how you tick. For some people, they are afraid of this exercise because they don't want to face the truth of who they are at that moment. But I ask you to realize that you must accept that we are all blank slates. And that is why we have the potential for greatness. We can make ourselves anything we want to be and nature has given us the best standing to leap from.

Believe in yourself and believe in your inspiration. Believe that whatever you need to make your inspiration a reality can be found around you. Believe that failure is a tool to learn and only temporary, but your decision to go on or quit is forever.

***

Chapter 5: Prejudice

"Prejudice is a burden that confuses the past, threatens the future and renders the present inaccessible."

Maya Angelou

We all hold some level of prejudice in any number of things at some station in our lives. We either underestimate something or overestimate it. Only hardly ever do we assign accurate understanding of something before we get to know it. That is the nature of all things when they come together for the first time.

The first time I got my dog from the pound, he was totally not what I expected; He turned out to be the sweetest thing that changed my life for the better. The first time I met my best boss, the first time I met my wife, the first time I met my business partner. They all turned out to be not what I thought of them when I first met them. The sets of people, who I thought were good, turned out to be great and the ones I thought were bad, turned out to be worse.

As I got older and wrested control of my thoughts from the hold of prejudices, I came to notice a pattern. My original thought was that I was a superb judge of character. You can clearly see why. Because the ones I thought were good, actually turned out to be great. However, I realized it was something more. The more I advanced and improved in clarity, thought and determination, I also noticed that *it wasn't the world that shaped my opinion of things; it was my opinion of things that shaped the world*. The pattern told me that I could make any relationship anyway I wanted it to be and even more, I could make any event or pursuit, anything I want it to be.

It was altogether the most astounding things that I came across because it bestowed three things on me.

I. The first was that I was the only one responsible for the way things unfolded for me.

II. The second was that I had the power to change things in my favor or even to turn any tide against me.

III. Finally, I found that the best way to look at anything is to look at it as means to reach my goals.

The three things I learned seemed to resemble each other under a different light, and in fact, they overlapped in many areas, as things of subtle nature often do. I had to make a choice of how to start seeing the positive in things so that they would impact me positively and in doing that, I found that I had to come to terms with what I believe. If I believed that something was bad for me, no matter how I tried to turn it or fake it, I couldn't until I changed what I believed. That, however, felt impossible to do until I found what was in plain sight all along.

To make every wave turn in my favor, I realized that everything that came my way came for a really good reason and they were all there to lift me up, not toss me down. Nothing that ever happened in my life since that time has resulted in catastrophe, neither have I sustained a defeat that I cannot rise from. I learned that by learning to truly believe in the whole, which is far much better than just trying to believe in just one small part.

If I am myopic then, it's hard to not be prejudiced. But when I see the big picture, my inspiration and all the things that come my way lock into place and only serve to do one thing - lead me to greatness, if I choose.

You can do this too. How it manifests in your life will differ from mine and sometimes, events will put your resolve through its paces but your belief should be able to rise above all forms of distractions. Your strength and your resolve will carry you in times of confusion and your meditation time will reinvigorate your moments of doubt with clearer view of your inspiration. You just have to remember to come back to your base. Stick to the innocent truth that no single event can bring you down; but put them all together and they are actually there to lift you up.

That's all you need to do. Once you believe in yourself, not only do you vanquish the army of the dark but you will get them to fight for you.

Once again, your armor against one of the distractions on your road to success is belief. You only need to remember one thing aside from the fact that you can use belief to conquer prejudice. You need to remember that you can use prejudice to locate and define the source of belief. It is a simple step, and the best way I can describe it is the way you would look at a large white sheet of paper that has a black dot on it. When we see that black dot, it is like us noticing the prejudice. But when we are forced to look at the white negative space around it, we suddenly realize that there is more to focus on than just that black dot. Belief is the same way. It is all around you, you just have to refocus.

***

Chapter 6: Negative Thoughts

"Believing in negative thoughts is the single greatest obstruction to success."

Charles F Glassman

I have met a large number of people in my life: All of them are really good people. Some are blessed with the natural ability to think positively. Some are blessed with the ability to be pragmatic, while a few have to battle the demons of negative thoughts that plague them on a daily basis.

In my own experience, I have not had a lot of negative thoughts, only a few, and I have never been one to really urge them on, or pursue them. I have always found them to be inaccurate and ultimately a waste of two precious resources - time and space in my conscious mind.

I suppose one of the reasons that negative thoughts and I don't really mix is because I choose to keep my mind engaged in the things that will advance my personal growth, and in the things that make me feel good. So as you can see, it was a natural mistake that at first, I thought that people with negative thoughts must feel horrible all day. Well, some do, and others don't. It has since become apparent to me that negative thoughts give comfort to people who are negative by nature.

Negative thoughts exist and persist in the mind of people who have found safe haven in those thoughts. At some deeper level, negative thoughts make excuses of all kinds and jive with the inherent nature of the person. They give you a multitude of reasons to not trust others and also give you reasons to not succeed and yet find it ok. They even give you reason to be abusive.

As you can tell, negative thoughts give you permission to be free in a dark sort of way. Once you fall into the trap of being negative, you find a treasure trove or excuses, prejudices, and fears in the outside world and only the cradle of negativity seems to keep you safe. When you keep the body safe, it rewards you with pleasure. However, this is pleasure based on an illusion.

The false pleasure that you get from the body gives you a plausible reason to not venture out to what needs to be done to succeed. Most people with negative thoughts are not consistently successful. They may succeed at this or that, here and there, especially in tasks that require a specific kind of energy and a certain amount of bravado. But other than that, they will always find it difficult to advance their success beyond this basket of deplorable feelings.

Vanquishing the Negative

The way to vanquish negative thoughts is not to attack them at all. You can never cease to allow negative thoughts inside as they sometimes flash in your mind. You must not disagree with them just as you must not agree with them. As far as negative thoughts are concerned, you have to completely disregard them when they come. A loud shout of **'NO!'** may help you whenever those thoughts come. You should never contemplate upon, or entertain them.

If you are the kind of person that is generally positive but you battle with negative thoughts occasionally, then the fix is simple. Imagine you are standing at the side of a freeway, where traffic is heavy but moving fast. Would you walk up and stand in front of any of those speeding vehicles? No, that would be catastrophic for you. Would you stand at the side of the road, and lock your sights on them and snap around as they pass you, then snap back and catch another vehicle and whip around as that one goes past? No. You will be in pain before long with all the snapping and whipping of your neck. Instead, the best way is to let each speeding vehicle just speed past. You don't have the power to engage them, and you don't have the resources to tame them to a halt, your best bet is to let them go on their way. Pretty soon, the volume of traffic dies down and you can get on your way.

But if you are the kind that finds pleasure in delving into the pool of negativity then you will always be attracted to those negative thoughts. Not only would you watch them constantly, you will attempt to jump in front of them and wrestle with them. This picture never ends so well because at that point, those negative thoughts become your beliefs and those beliefs influence your actions and pretty soon otherwise innocuous thoughts turn to destructive actions.

The best way to counter negative thoughts, especially if you are the second kind, is to be able to engage in mindfulness and discipline yourself every time you feel a negative thought coming on, or you seek the shelter of a negative thought. Then you need to begin a breathing exercise that shifts your focus from those speeding thoughts to your own breathing. For those of you who have frequently repeating negative thoughts, you have to discipline yourself to trigger a kind of reaction where you begin to turn to this breathing exercise as soon as you feel a negative thought coming on. This takes discipline.

To be able to do all these, you need to also come to the realization that all this while that you have been dealing with negative thoughts, things have not been going as good as they should have. If you look deep in your heart you will know this to be true and the way out is not to reflect on more negativity, but to turn to positivity and believe that your life is more than just a series of defensive negative maneuvers. If you find out that your support system is populated with people who are negative, it's time that you extricated yourself from this group and if you have to be alone, so be it. Better yet, **GET NEW FRIENDS**. Leave the negative thoughts and negative influences behind.

You need a new chapter in your life where you believe in the whole, not the parts. This world is not made up of individual seemingly bad encounters: It is made up with good in its entirety. You're just focusing on the bad and your negativity and negative thoughts magnify it. Once you discipline yourself to look away, you will find that you can dictate whether the things that happen to you are positive or negative.

You need to embrace the power of belief and internalize the matrix of belief to have a rebirth from the negative thoughts you have. A friend of mine that I know well, suffered from these negative thoughts since he was a teenager. What brought them to the surface, I do not know. But by the time he was in his thirties, they dictated his thoughts, his behavior and his station in life - which was very poor indeed. When he was thirty-eight, he started meditating to relieve the stresses that were mounting from the negative thoughts, and slowly over the course of three years, his path altered. Without any medication or professional psychological help, he managed to turn things around. He is in his fifties now and has filed more than 18 patents in his name for the inventions that he came up with. If you ask him what his secret was, as I have, his answer is simple. It's just that he started to believe in himself

***

Chapter 7: Pleasing Others

"You are not supposed to set yourself ablaze to keep others warm."

Anonymous

It is a common trait among human beings to please others. It is rooted in the fact that we are social beings - creatures that thrive well in society rather than in isolation. Hence, the tendency is for us to cooperate. Sometimes that sense of cooperation overflows its boundaries and we end up with self-sacrifice - where it is a one-way street of giving to the point of our own detriment. That is not required of us.

But the real problem comes when you do not believe in yourself and you think that you need to be nice to others so that in the event you are in trouble, you can lean on them for assistance. It doesn't work that way.

The real desire of wanting to please others is so that they will come to like you and that affirmation that they send your way may, in some way, help you feel better about yourself. It doesn't work that way either.

The reason society works is not that you want to please others, or that you spend your life serving others, instead, society works because there is a social contract that says, '*I do this, and you do that in return*'. We have since monetized one person's efforts so that another person can assign a value to it and then pay for it.

If you find that you have the inexplicable desire to please people, then it's time you stopped and asked yourself "*What is the level of my belief in my own abilities, my own existence, and my own life?*" You need to find the answer to this because of the fact that you are trying to constantly please others for nothing.

You can ask for help, that is not a sign of weakness. You can ask for assistance, and you can fail, yet none of these are signs of weakness. You can even fail over and over again. Even that is not a sign of weakness. But the moment you just decide to please people then you need to alert yourself to a weakness that is coming to the surface and what you have to do is find the source and end it.

Lao Tzu, a Chinese philosopher, says that '*if you are trying to please people, you will always be their slave*'. And whether you realize it or not, you already know it. Maybe not consciously, but you know it at a very deep level, and you know it since the prevailing mindset of those who are subservient is that they are protected by the master. That's the typical relationship between master and servant. When you try to please people, you are in search of their protection. But there is no point when they do not know it. In the end, you are the loser.

So the question then remains, "Why do you need protection?" The reason you subconsciously need protection is that you are in the state of fear. You do not believe that you are able to get to the point in your life that you have in your head, or in worst case scenario, you do not believe in your own abilities. This is not just a question of self-doubt or self-esteem, it's about you having zero belief in your ability to carry out your purpose in life, and you cede control to anyone who would take it.

If this is you, then there is one thing working in your favor. The answer lies in the problem. It is almost always the case that all solutions depend on the problem and are found within it if you look hard enough. The fact that you need to please people tells you that you need to resolve that by learning how to believe in yourself - that includes learning to believe in the universe and your soul's oneness with it, your belief in your body and its purpose, and your belief in your mind. When you realize this, you realize that you can be anything you want to be without ever having to be pliant to another's will.

Belief is a strong ally. If you learn to believe in the universe and your place in it, then the law of attraction instantly starts working for you. But if you stay oblivious to your own greatness then the law of the universe is still going to work, but not in the way you would want.

Up till this point, you have seen the seven shades of belief. It has been presented to you as the distractions you face on the path to success. That is totally accurate, but what is at a deeper level is the fact that belief takes on many shades and dimensions and can fit the core of your being in a way that is able to fend off every single one of the distractions you have seen in this book.

Belief is a multi-faceted, multi-dimensional state of yourself. It feels like a feeling and it is spoken of here as a tool, but it really is a state that you become with practice and one day you wake up and all the things that once plagued you, listed in the chapter of this book here, are no longer dictating your thoughts, guiding your hand, or obscuring your purpose.

The key to all you do is the belief that you are more than the sum of your parts, and you are more than perishable tissue and thoughts. You are the vessel of inspiration and you can do anything if you want.

***

Chapter 8: Negative Environment

"Surround yourself with positive souls, and positive vibes will come naturally. Your environment influences your experience. Make it a positive one."

Anonymous

We may find ourselves situated in a negative environment in a number of ways. The environment can either be impressed upon you without you having any say in it, or it could also be that circumstances led you to this negative environment. Or you just gravitated towards it because you felt safe in the company of non-achievers.

There are probably a number of other ways to get into negative environments but that doesn't matter. There is always a root cause that gets you, and there is a similar root cause for the fact that you can't seem to find your way out once you are in.

Before we visit the nature of this true cause, let's look a little at what a negative environment does to you.

The human psyche is such that it conforms to societal pressures. We dare not step outside the societal norms and we feel that it is better to belong to something negative than to go out into the cold alone. Negative environments are ones wherein you find yourself in the company of a group that influences your societal values and you end up having to behave in some of the same ways that your negative friends behave.

Imagine what it would feel like if you were in a crooked town where all the city officials took kickbacks and bribes. You walk in one day and suddenly you find that you are the only one not doing it. That is a negative culture and it is one that will start to have negative effects on you.

We all get into these environments. It's how kids get into gangs and go down the wrong path; it's the route some adults take and end up doing things they regret.

Consequences aside, negative environments are usually the result of a budding or non-existent belief in self. If you do not believe in your own resources and your own inspirations, then you are going to congregate with others who harbor the same state of mind, and that becomes unhealthy. At best, you become mediocre in your life, at worst case you turn to *gangsterism* and a life of crime. Negative environments are breeding grounds for the worst in us because we are emboldened by numbers and negativity in numbers becomes a horrific weapon.

You need to evaluate who you spend your time with, and who has your ear. As Shakespeare writes, *"Give every man thy ear, but few thy voice"* He was essentially asking everyone to refrain from judging people or taking the positions of other men. But you can only do that when you believe that your place in this world is true and that your ability in this world is beyond doubt.

The way out of this is to stand firm on your set of beliefs and take charge of what goes on around you. Since you cannot change people or your environments, the thing you have to do is move. Never let yourself stay in an environment that is negative. Never let yourself be swayed by the negative vibes of your surroundings. You can only hold on to your beliefs for so long and then, trust me; they will start to mimic their environment. So you need to move out of it and you need to find silence in your life while you detox from the negative environments.

One thing that you should inquire is the reason you gravitated to that environment in the first place. Your beliefs need to be positive or pragmatic about yourself. At the local level, belief is best understood if applied pragmatically. At the global stage, belief should be entirely positive.

The way it works is that you have to be pragmatic about where you are, and who you are. What your shortfalls are and what you need to improve on. You can only get that when you are pragmatic.

Whenever you look at the global scene and when you look at the universe, you must see that it is positive. What you see should be that the universe is giving you everything. The universe will give you whatever you ask for and so when you desire the best, you will get the opportunity to be the best. That's the good you can believe in, and that's positive.

***

Chapter 9: Fear of Success

One of the strangest distractions that is present on the path to success, is the actual fear of success itself. We all know how to daydream about the Italian villa which we plan to jet off to in the summer: Or how we could change the world to be a better place modeled according to our own personal beliefs.

There are so many dreams that we get. Many of those dreams have nothing to do with the inspiration that we get. Many of those dreams are really pies in the sky and they are not real. We are not inspired by such dreams as we are just trying to imagine what we see on TV, what we read in magazines, and what we assume the successful people live like.

Much of this fear is driven by pride, some of it by ego, and some of it can even be driven by laziness. We are so lazy at times that we think to ourselves that if we can hit one big success, we can live like kings for the rest of our lives.

It's no wonder when our definition of success is so warped, that we are subconsciously afraid of it because at a deep level, we know there is no basis in what we are fantasizing about.

When our inspiration is just fantasy - and these are unreal fantasies at that, our subconscious raises our levels of fear because the failure would be catastrophic from these lofty heights of fantasy.

The only way to shatter this fear of success is to be able to sweep all these unrealistic fantasies away and then start focusing on real inspiration. Once you focus on real inspiration you can start to believe in it. As you apply your discipline towards the tasks while you believe in the inspiration, success will slowly but surely show up.

Fear of success can also be the result of the fear of the unknown. If you have never gained much success, the first time you arrive at it, you will be instantly afraid. It is because the body naturally fears what it doesn't know and the change in your state that is about to happen is unchartered territory for your body. It throws up fear as a response stimuli.

In this case, belief is also the answer. When you believe that the universe always sends across good things, no matter how it is packaged, then you will be able to surmount the fear.

***

Chapter 10: Focusing on the Rewards

The biggest distraction there is to reaching success is when one chooses to focus on the rewards exclusively. Rewards that are material are meant for the body to enjoy, and when you fantasize about such rewards, you're actually distracting your mind from achieving a greater goal. But of course, there are times to psyche yourself up. There are times it's nice to look at the goal from a reward perspective, but you can't always do that. In fact, your inspiration should not be fueled by the rewards that you think you can get from attaining the success.

Focusing on the rewards is a clear sign that you need to artificially inflate your energy to attain the success. You may hit the mark once or twice but you won't be able to keep that up. The biggest reason is that the rewards you dream of, are not as great in reality when you actually get it.

When you dream of getting your first Ferrari, for instance, the dream is intense and is very palpable. You can't wait for it, you work hard, you go all out, and finally, the day arrives when you can afford it; you order it, you pick it up and you're driving it, and within a few days, you realize it's just another car.

Don't get me wrong, it's a great car, especially once you learn how to drive it. But the reason it's not that great after a while is that nothing in this world can ever live up to the hype of your fantasy.

When this happens after a few times, you are left with the realization that there is nothing that seems to live up to the fantasy and so there is no fuel in your tank to go after success, after all, the rewards never meet the expectation.

The only way to go after success is to believe that success is its own reward. When you beat the odds, when you realize that the universe is on your side; when you hit one success after the other consecutively, the reward is so great that no physical reward, no monetary gain, no supercar can every replace it. Even though you would probably be able to afford everything you ever dreamed of, it won't matter, you will be too busy being successful.

***

Conclusion

Belief is an integral component of success. Without belief, you may sputter on your way and you will most times fall short of the excellence mark without an understanding of the reasons behind your shortfall. Belief is the antidote for so many of your path's distractions, and before you can even get to your destination, the lack of belief will leave you exposed to numerous pitfalls and delusions.

Belief is also not the definition of getting swindled. I have come to realize that most people think that it is smarter to be pessimistic or doubtful of all things, and that way you can be cautious just in case some things that need caution, arise. However, you can't be cautious about everything. You cannot worry over some inevitable occurrences, for example a thief coming in the night to steal your car, or you can't be worried whether a financial crisis will erode your wealth after you've built it. That is not the kind of belief we are talking about.

Belief is about looking at yourself and saying that you are able to reach the heights of success that you've dreamed of. Belief is about you harnessing your inspiration and saying, *"Yes, I can do that"* without any visible evidence that points to that fact. You believe because your inspiration placed it there.

At the age of six, my father took me to an air show at the airbase where he worked. It was the first time I had seen planes up close. We sat in them; we walked around them; we spoke to the pilots; we watch the aerial display; and I went home that night fascinated. From that day on, I dreamt everyday - literally, of becoming a pilot. I read about planes whenever I could. I collected photographs every chance I got, and I even drew airplanes in my free time. I even drew the layout of a cockpit, pasted it at the head of my bed, and imagined I was flying. The idea of being a pilot so inspired me that it filled me up without a doubt whatsoever that I would one day become a pilot.

My life as an adult took me across a different path. One that was more mature where I had responsibilities and being a pilot would not have worked out with those responsibilities hanging on my neck. Hence, I continued on with other successes in my life until I got to the point where I could get my pilot's license privately. Something that struck me when I was just six, materialized less than 30 years later in a way that was even better than I had imagined, and it never even felt like I put the effort into it. It just happened.

There were many things in my life that happened that way, and there were many things in my life that I had to work hard for, many things that I failed at, many things I lost, many times I picked myself up and had to do it again, but all while, I believed that whatever happened in my life happened to raise me up and never to push me down.

That belief always paid off for me. That belief gave me strength to go against the crowd. It has always given me extra strength to do things that were not the norm and the strength to believe in myself because, after all, I had the universe backing me.

In many cases, people have stopped dreaming because some fool told them that *'those are all pies in the sky'* and that they needed to get their head out of the clouds and get their noses back to the grindstone. You cannot dream your way to the top. Getting to the top requires hard work that is consistently applied and championed by a firm will.

***

Epilogue

The destination you have reached is not just the end of the book on belief and how to detect the lack of it in yourself. You have come to the end of the five-part series on success. Success is not to be trifled with, it is serious business and it deserves an understanding. The understanding that you need is not so much the definition of terms and concepts, but more importantly you need to see where you are in the grand scheme of things. Success is a personal endeavor. It is as personal as your retinal pattern, as personal as your DNA encoding, and your thumbprint.

Success for me is the achievement of something that will be very different compared to what your success is going to be. That's one of the reasons we can't really quantify success in commoditized terms. Mother Teresa attained greatness and success through very different means than Winston Churchill. Mahatma Gandhi attained greatness very differently from Christopher Columbus. Even contemporary greats like Steve Jobs did it differently compared to Alan Turing.

The kind of success you see in yourself when you soul is burning with the fire called inspiration, will dictate the hand that makes it a reality. But if you begin to define your success by the measure of someone else's yardstick, you will never measure up. You cannot measure the height of a blade of wheat with the benchmark of a giant redwood.

What is important for you to succeed is that you look at your own inspiration and then go out and get it. Or if you really want to do something that's different, you can even cogitate your path and then ask for inspiration to make it happen. Whichever way you choose, the path is long and fraught with distractions.

The one consolation you can take from this is that those distractions will come from within you, and from those close to you. That is where your strength needs to shine and your belief needs to remain firm.

This book represents the last in the series of five, but in no way should that make a difference to you. This book was designed to be repeatedly read. The material that defines the nature of success is spread across the books and not in any methodical fashion. Success is not a series of steps you follow. It is a series of steps you make.

My sincere suggestion is that you read each book, in successive turn and then go back to read them again. Some concepts and analogies are mentioned in one book and then talked about in another. It may seem confusing the first time around, but that's only because I have tried my best to not repeat any of the material, leaving more space for fresh material. Describing such a voluminous topic in just five books and across a combined five hundred pages requires a lot of condensing. But it's all here, rest assured. If you take the time to read them all over again, and again, you will begin to not just understand the material, but you will start to feel it resonate deep down.

Once you internalize the material, you can get on your way to using it.

With that said, I will leave you with the timeless words of William Ernest Henley.

Invictus
by William Ernest Henley

Out of the night that covers me,
Black as the Pit from pole to pole,
I thank whatever gods may be
For my conquerable soul.

In the fell clutch of circumstance
I have not winced nor cried aloud
Under the bludgeoning of chance
My head is bloody, but unbowed.

Beyond the place of wrath and tears
Looms but the horror of the shade
And yet the menace of the years
Finds, and shall find, me unafraid.

It matters not how straight the gate,
How charged with punishment the scroll,
I am the master of my fate;
I am the captain of my soul.

***

Make sure to check out the rest of the books in this series:

Fail Your Way to Success: The Definitive Guide to Failing Forward and Learning How to Extract the Greatness Within - Why Failing is an Integral Part of Success and Why You Should Never Fear it

https://www.amazon.com/dp/B0738WDK6W

Discipline Your Way to Success: The Definitive Guide to Success Through Self-Discipline - Why Self-Discipline is Crucial to Your Success Story and How to Take Control Over Your Thoughts and Actions

https://www.amazon.com/dp/B0741FMCRX

Meditate Your Way to Success: The Definitive Guide to Mindfulness, Focus and Meditation - How Meditation is an Integral Part of Success and Why You Should Get Started Now

https://www.amazon.com/dp/B073ZMCHQJ

Ask Your Way to Success: The Definitive Guide to Success Through Asking - How to Transform Your Life by Learning the Art of Asking

https://www.amazon.com/dp/B074CJPFMH

www.ingramcontent.com/pod-product-compliance
Lightning Source LLC
Chambersburg PA
CBHW021135300426
44113CB00006B/432